Covid 19

Morbid

Sordid

Torrid

By

Deluke Muwanigwa

COPYRIGHT @ 2021 COVID 19 MORBID SORDID TORRID
by Deluke Muwanigwa

All rights reserved. No part of this publication may be reproduced, distributed, or transmitted in any form or any means, including photocopying, recording, or other electronic or mechanical methods without the prior written permission of the publisher and author, excerpt in the case of brief quotations embodied in critical reviews and certain other non-commercial uses permitted by copyright law. For permission requests, write to the publisher at <u>lovelypoetess95@gmail.com</u>.

.

Published by Poetry Planet Book Publishing House
Arranged by Tess Ritumalta
ISBN;
Softbound/Paperback-978-621-8261-80-8
Hardbound-978-621-8261-81-5
Mobile/Kindle-978-621-8261-82-2

Photos used were taken from Pinterest and may contain their own copyrights

DEDICATION

This book is dedicated to all the unfortunate people whose lives were cut short by Covid 19. I hope with more vaccination, and strict following of Covid 19 rules, those who recovered or were not affected will continue to enjoy good health. Covid 19 has shown us that we are humans first before any belief or ethnicity. Hopefully, this will increase our attitudes towards each other. Keep safe and enjoy the poetry.

PREFACE

Wear a mask, sanitize and practice social distancing. I made good use of the time in quarantine to write this and other poems. The poems in this book are not all about Covid 19, for want of variety. I hope you enjoy reading these poems in spite of the subject being morbid, sordid, and torrid.

TABLE OF CONTENTS

FELLOW HUMANS

Fellow humans
I bid you goodbye
This is not a good lie
I'm leaving for mars
Going with all my scars
To live among the stars
Am leaving all my cars

Fellow humans
Look what you done
Earth is no longer fun
It's become unlivable
The intolerance unbelievable
The suffering unbearable
The poverty intolerable

Fellow humans
I'm ready to live alone
Far away without a phone
The virus called COVID
Made our lives torrid
Our world morbid
Our funerals sordid

Fellow humans
I'm riding Star Dragon soon
Will whizz past the moon

Thank you Elon Musk
Am leaving my face mask
Building a colony my new task
No one to miss me or ask

COVID ON STREET 2.0

A parking cashier sauntered to my car carrying a swipe machine, a face mask, and a pleasant smile I could only imagine was behind the mask-of- fear-of-contagion. A pretty young lass I imagined must have got her job due to her stunning African beauty, which I noted nonchalantly. My mind wondered how young girls were wooed these days when they are forced to cover their most marketable asset; the face. Then my daft think box realized technology has overtaken the good old system of stolen moments at parties, discos, and the movies. Now it's WhatsApp, Facebook, etc. I thought, thank God human beings always find a way even in the dark days of Covid 19!

I had USD on me, no local currency notes. Our schizophrenic government pretends all was well. There are not enough USD notes and worse still local notes, but people have migrated to using bitcoin called EcoCash. Due to the shortage of cash, a thriving market of electronic cash has spawned unbridled money markets whose deleterious effects may yet unseat the powers that be. Bureaucracy blames everyone else except themselves. As usual.

I digress. So, I had USD; she had no change. I had no local notes, she had a swipe machine for bitcoin. Sigh! I was stuck because if I didn't pay for parking my car it would be clamped and I would have to dig deep in my empty shallow pockets to have my car released. Clamping fees are so high you can get a cardiac arrest. As usual in these sticky situations, I unstuck myself by phoning the mother of my kids. My saviourimean, my second one after Jesus Christ. Instantly I got wired money on my phone and paid using Ecocash; a popular platform giving the Reserve Bank a run for their money. As providence had it, I had also forgotten my swipe card which I share with my queen. In all this, social distancing and hand sanitizing were on the back burner, while we haggled over parking fees. I'm sure SAR COV 2 was lurking not far with its invisible scalpel. When I raised my head from the payment fiasco I was struck by the all-pervasive message on billboards, shop fronts, and car stickers. "Be Wise Sanitize", screamed the warning. I thought, welcome to hell bro!

I lost count of how many roadblocks I had gone through on a stretch of 12kms. The uniformed forces clad in their infamous uniforms of repression were stopping every vehicle to demand travel permits. You had to have documentation to prove that you were on a Covid mission or had a letter from your local officer in charge of police to justify your being up and about. As usual, many went past by dropping a dollar. I even drove through without a license which I had forgotten with an overzealous police officer at another roadblock. With the police focusing on Covid 19, I drive without a driver's license these days because they are focused on

Covid 19. I doubt the offices that issue replacement licenses are functional anywhere.

The few cars able to penetrate the roadblocks drove slowly. I drove slowly, more an instinctive subconscious decision due to the preponderous of police and army. Drivers seemed to be socially distancing due to the police "virus". There was a beeline of idling cars spewing their ozone-depleting toxins at a petrol station. Above the din of idling cars was a deeper roar of diesel generators everywhere. I suspected there was no grid power. This was a daily occurrence due to a severe drought that had depleted the waters of the Zambezi River from where most electricity was generated. In fact, most people were resorting to renewable energy to supplement erratic utility power. In fact, this was the cause of my visit to town. I was looking for a solar panel and pump for irrigating my crop at my farm plot.

So, here I was facing Covid and the uniformed officers in the city. Everywhere it said, " Be wise Sanitized".

So far, I think, I have been wise. I have sanitized.

A CRIME

It's a crime to write a poem without a rhyme
Those that say nay pray that the god of poetry spare
you
For what use is the blunderbuss if the gunpowder be
slime
Those that say yea years of ale will be bestowed upon
you it's true
Those that rhyme a couplet may you live long
Like the love of Juliet, a Capulet was strong
Those that rhyme other forms as long as they rhyme be
blessed
Like the Jewish doctrine still fervently practiced in the
Knesset
So, go forth and create those beautiful words
Take the poem, the imaginary, and the metaphor to
other worlds
Do not be economical with that forced rhyme
It is better to clutch at straws than commit a crime
For, with a poetic license from the god of poetry, who
says dilemma,
Must not, will not rhyme "dial her ma"

1918.......AGAIN

I am here watching the horror, wondering whether I'll be next, or you or them. My mind wanders to Chimoio, to Nyadzonia after the aluminum birds, Canberra, bat-shaped Vampire, the aristocratic Hawk Hunter, dropped their toxic eggs. Napalm! Incendiary! "Aluoette je te plumari". I see her hovering over the smelling dead and dying bodies finishing off the living dead. Pumping tons of copper and bronze pellets into a new mine that never was. Escorting the enemy on one side, the freedom fighter on the other, the refugee in the middle, to oblivion! Deaths are us!

The preacher man sitting on the right side of his father has gone quiet. His thoughts macabre. He looks to his left to seek divine counsel. There is a stone statue where his father sat. Stone cold. Stone silence. He watches his flock of sheep convulse and expire. Hopeless, helpless. Perhaps the Book needs a second reading. Faith losing face. There is a big bang in his head. Perhaps the scientist is right, he muses in despair. Who is right? WHO?

Leaders now a masquerade. Talking political Swahili through a mask. No one pays attention. Puppets on a string. Ideologues without ideology. Looking after their need. Scared to lead. Are they still real or are they themselves shaking in their boots, thinking of their roots, their ancestors?

Loudest silence at rallies. For the led, tears run dry. Vocal cords are broken. Crying is a luxury. Do I sense a smile on the soulless faces? All races. Equanimity in calamity. The rich dead. The poor living another day having nothing to say, no one to pay.

Perhaps we are shooting spaceships into the galaxies in vain. The pain is here. The rain will not save us. Seasons come with no reason to celebrate. The young celibate. Partners are socially distanced, mass lepers of a lost world. ET is here. We can't see it. Know they are here. Spherical balls with spikes and only 2 DNA strands. Amoeba. Paramecium. The bigger we get the smaller the enemy. WHO is the enemy?

Covid 19.1918.......again.

A HUMAN BEING

The most beautiful thing on earth is a human being
Given just enough sense and intelligence to hate
another human being
Just because he crossed the river of life
He opens floodgates of acid water to make sure others
never cross the Nile
Full of stratagems even music is biased in favour of him
Full of strategy even religion conjured up complete with
a hymn
While one is busy reading fiction shutting their eyes to
visualize the deity
The cunning is busy doing science stealing riches playing
dirty.

He has enough brainpower to love a flower
Not enough sympathy empathy to know every mother
carries his brother
Praying to the god of politics as if it's a religion
kowtowing to fascist racists
Playing with weapons of mass extinction, toys deploying
a ploy by narcissists
Bending the truth to acquire dominance
Signing a truce only to achieve prominence
The most beautiful thing on earth is a human being
Given just enough sense and intelligence to hate
another human being for being

THE LONE JOURNEY

All alone among many
Didn't start today
This I have to say
Billions swam with me
I was not free
In my father's loins
I was still lonely
Cutthroat competition
I don't want a repetition

Even my progenitor
The careless impregnator
Sometimes sitting around a fire
Man spreading us to hell
My swimmers dying I could tell
Then he would bath in ice
That too wasn't right
I won the race of life
To be stuck alone in a lake so tight
Without rights

Then my incubator
My mom was no better
When I saw the entrance
I was in outrage
Instead of helping me along
She was crying and writhing long

When my head was out
Is the only time I could shout
Only to find a brood of evil dressed in white
And I thought this is not right

The loneliness continued
Even got renewed
My competitor siblings
They would always be dribbling
Many times I would get punished
Something I didn't do felt like banished
When I came of age
This got worse and strange
I was happier alone
Having nothing to atone

Got me a wife
For the rest of my life
Many years of fondness
Turning to loneliness
There are things obvious you thought
In reality misery they brought
You get lonely
Hopefully you only
The futility of community
Affecting your mental immunity

So, I laugh in derision
At your unfortunate decision
To abandon me

You see
I am alone
Even at home
Even out there
People never fair
Life is a lone journey
A lone journey for many

A THOUSAND APOLOGIES

To all the poets offended by me
I wanna offer a thousand apologies
Perhaps you don't rhyme and I said its a crime
If you believed its a crime then you got no sense of
humor
Lighten up it was a poet playing with words in jest
If my anti-religion rhetoric offended the pious I
apologize
However, think deep and look at the history of injustice
There is a common thread creating differences among
people based on political boundaries reinforced by
religion
Not any particular religion but ALL religions
To those offended by my comments on their poems,
apologies again
I know some treat their work like newborn babies
Sorry to have criticized your baby's colour, shape of the
nose, ears, and ethnic etymology
It's also quite possible I came across as I know it all
narcissist. Am I bad?
I'm just a common guy blessed with a beautiful family
and most of my poems are make-believe.
So, Fellow Humans, forgive a brother.
After all, I am leaving for mars, with my scars, and
leaving all my cars.
Enjoy your poetry and don't let anyone dissuade you
from self-expression.

A RECORD

Good morning World
Good morning Zimbabwe
I know things are hard for all of us
But there's nothing like waking up to a new day
Another day another life
Forget your angst for a moment
Forget your snarky negative comment
And just think some as of yesterday died
Some as of yesterday at funerals cried
But you the chosen one
Have another day of fun
Go on run
Write that pun
You are chosen
My cousin
Wherever you are
No matter how far
Spread the love
Let it come
It is beautiful to be alive
To finally arrive
At this day
I say
At this hour
Life is ours
This minute
I mean it

This second
A record

DO YOU?

Do you remember a time and place?
I did not have a face
My erstwhile lover
Undercover
You felt my nakedness
Not negativeness

Do you remember a time and place?
The bliss
Of my kiss
You knew in blindness
I knew your kindness
Knowledge is power
Yours wilted the flower

Do you remember a time and place?
I was perfection
Per action
Our souls met
A perfect match
Now your doubt
Is loud
It's too late
You have had a taste
Of the forbidden
You can't be forgiven

Do remember a time and place?
We willingly both
Took a blood oath
It is done
Can't be undone

Now you know my face
Steps you can't retrace
To a time and place
A time and place

AFRIKA!

Went round to Westgate Shopping Centre
grudgingly to deposit money back to the sender
The crooked banker capitalist tycoons
ripping your life savings like a typhoon
I parked my little Fit Honda Jazz,
walked to the bank entrance unfazed

A big burly bully guard shook his head,
pointing at his chin. "No entry! ", he said
Bollicks! I had forgotten my face mask
"Can I use the lapel of my tee-shirt? ", I asked
Goliath shook his head, hand on baton stick
Said I was adding on to people getting sick
I went to a flea market to buy a face contraption
And was allowed in by BBBG without interruption.

Our first Covid wave killed about two hundred.
Most came with the disease from overseas to see
kindred
Some already dying with terminal diseases
People here are relaxed scoffing at rules with teases
So even Engineer DM with all his supposed education
left home without a mask and with BBBG had an
altercation.

They say a second wave is definitely coming
We are still waiting for the first wave running

There is a scientific reason why we Negros in Africa
weathered the storm better than people in Antarctica
Scientists are baffled, haters and racists disappointed
Whatever it is this time around we are the chosen race,
anointed

God is great Africa!
Allahu akbar Afrika!

AFTER TWENTY-ONE DAYS

After twenty-one days
No time to be in a daze
Two of us have work to do
We've to start the world anew
Corona will kill everyone
COWrona kill cattle everywhere
There'll be only goat meat
Goats walking on every street
We will burn all the dead people
All of them strong or feeble
Homes will be crematoria
People will be in purgatoria

After twenty-one days
There'll be nothing to say
Just the two of us alone
No one else to phone
People dead from Cairo to cape
All tribes will not escape
We had all the bombs
The military, the vigilante mobs
The enemy we couldn't see
He didn't hide behind a tree
The enemy lived in your chest
Took your breath till you rest

After twenty-one days
Doesn't matter what anybody says
We will build a hut in one day
There will be no time to pray
We will have to find food
We will create our own mood
You cast away your gown
No one is there to look down
They are all dead and gone
We are completely on our own
You have me and I have you
We have to start the world anew
After twenty-one days...

AGAIN AND AGAIN

A man is born alone
Finds life forlorn
Life a big groan
Mortgaged home
Burden of loans
Bill's on the phone
Constantly moans
Clothes all torn
Dies on his own
Despite the pain
He wants to be born again and again

He tried
He cried
'But why? '
He sighed
He lied
Defied
Decried
Even implied
He eyed
But died
It's insane
He wants to be born again and again

The refrain remains
He wants to be born again and again

ALL CONTINENTS

On the oscillograph of life
Alone going up and down there's strife
Blood pressure high and low
Dot on cathode ray going slow

On the big oscillograph accurate
Remote palpitations undulate
Blood sugar above and below
Reading on chart dangerously low

On the big world LOVE-O-GRAM
One heartbeat one love on Instagram
All systems settled to standard
Dots synchronized together bandied

Spread the love, spread the love
And happiness
Spread the health, spread health
And healthiness
One oscillograph, one oscillograph
Synchronized heartiness
All over the world, spread the love.
On all continents.

ALL LIVES MATTER

All lives matter
What you did not create
Do not render asunder

All lives matter
What you cause a threat
God strikes you with thunder

All lives matter
What you have met
God loves even down under

All lives matter
What you can bet
Take your 666 number

Don't take His position
And end another's life
Because All Lives Matter

ALONE IN INDIA

Last week I was in India visiting friends
I went to the Pink City with Fred
as the City of Jaipur is popularly known
In the State of Rajasthan, it felt like home

We drove down Mahal Road in a "tempo"
Visited Amer Fort and Janta Mantar temples
Next day went to the City Palace
Beautiful people speaking Hindi and Marwari.
We drove past Suresh Gyan Vihar University sanctuary
Then stopped at Phatak marketplace
teeming with people moving at a fast pace

Our "tempo" took us to World Trade Park
An upper-class mall we shopped till dark
From Malvina Nagar to Gaurav Nagar the next day
At GT Bazaar we shopped till we had no money to pay

The town of Jaitpura was so pleasant
Nice friendly people, the rich, the poor, and the
peasants
India is such a welcoming country and feels like a
second home
Next stop Southern Kartanaka State and this time I go
alone

ARE YOU NOT INSANE?

I am crawling in the streets of my brain.
Avoiding polluting the delicate frame
I am looking for something
What I find is not nothing

Electric cables
Eclectic fables
Billions of synapsis
Trillions of lapses

What a mess
What a maze
Unknown Junctions
Unknown functions

Rivers of blood
Juices in flood
Ideas in mud
Creating a dud

Swelling
Smelling
Spelling
Quelling

A real conundrum
A real cone in a drum
No wonder things never make sense
No wonder dreams yield nonsense

I have a headache
I have a heartache
Maybe it's a heartburn
Heart pains, head burns

I am crawling out of my brain
before I cause a mental strain
But I m already seeing things
Frightening earthly beings

Mouths in the rear
Eyes queer queer
Is it not too late for me?
Can I forget where I've been?

I don't know anymore
My brain is so very sore
I can't focus
Everything bogus

I see a country with a nasty ruler
I see a nation with a wheeler-dealer
Africans living in Wuhan in Siberia
Dominicans in Sichuan in Liberia

I can't take the changes
I can't fake its strange
I have got to get out
I have to go shout

Arghhhhhhhh! ! ! ! ! ! ! ! ! ! !
Arghhhhhhhh! ! ! ! ! ! ! ! ! ! ! !

What about you?
Will you tell the truth?
What's in your brain?
Are you not insane?

ARE YOU STILL THERE?

I am searching for you deep in my heart
I hope you have not decided to depart
From this old heart of mine
This my old heart so so fine
I hope you are still there
wandering its thoroughfare
You are my star
don't go far

Dwell within it for eternity
It will give you paternity
give you maternity
The right ventricle for me and you
The left for our tots born anew
Our kids
Our seeds
For their needs

I will never bleed
Unless you decide to leave
Breaking this heart of ours
blood flowing for hours
don't go away my flower
You give me the willpower
to search for you everywhere
In my heart of hearts are you still there?

BACK TO MY ROOTS

Poetry is self-expression
Whereas some want to give a different impression
It is best to be spontaneous
To achieve something momentous I used to write well
Now I am on a dry spell
Reading too many styles
Bringing smiles
But scattering my art
To doubt me, I start

It is good to read other works
To measure your worth
But experiences are different Command of language
different Personalities different
Differences different

I have to go back to my roots
Wear my original poetic boots
And write and write and write
Even when they say my poems are not right.
I will let my poems take flight
Write what I want into the night.

'Way back from Geoffrey Chaucer, there had been much change in style form and everything. There is Victorian poetry, romantic poetry, modernist poetry, etc...even in sonnets, there is Petrarchan sonnet and Shakespearean sonnet with a difference. Many poetries cannot be put in any of forms, but still, they exist...do just enjoy your poetic style and vibe.

But you say you just write poetry. It has nothing to do with self-expression...'

BAILOUT

There is light at the end of the tunnel
A tunnel-shaped like a funnel
By the time you get to the end
Will the time tunnel extend?
It's opening
For your rude awakening

Turn back!
Don't make the mistake
The little that you have, you have
Be brave
Work hard
In the mud
There's gold
Untold
The manna
On the other side is manual

Voyages of discovery
For your recovery
Never-ending, Never!
Be clever.
Send probes
Send strobes
What you thought was something
It May turn out to be nothing

Your nemesis is in the air
It's there
Breathe in breathe out
Feel the bout.
Don't doubt
The rout
The clout
Bailout.

MY HEART IS BURNING SO COLD

Someone ignited freezing coals
My heart is beating fast with zero pulse
Zapped with zero volts of electrical impulse
I think my hyperactive brain is in a comma
My labyrinth of thoughts failing every corner
I am feeling lonely in eight billion
Hidden out in the open changing colours a million
I feed my hunger to starvation
My energy radiating out to feed my deprivation
Those who used care
They stand there, stare
Those who loved
They succumbed
What do I do now?
To live I don't know-how
I am as happy as a star
I will never bear a scar
Going back to my element
Basic elements
Calcium
Carbon
Dead
End.

BEAST MODE (limerick)

In a twist, Clint rode east with Yeast in beast mode
In the mist, the horse went up and downhill it rode
His gun a four four
His gun hand so sore
He emptied other's gun as hombre snored

Beast mode

B-e still Children of God
E-ven as you search for gold
A-nd real estate
S-top! Don't escalate
T-o your neighbour
M-artial ways, abhor!
O-nly leadership
D-efeats brinkmanship
E-ast Mode not beast mode

Beast mode

Cryptically decrypt critical beast mode
Talk walk folk don't stalk baulk
Share fair rare welfare austere square
TikTok Talk tick itch flick switch stitch
No rat a tat tat tat tat rat a tat tat tat
Talk talk talk talk talk walk the talk talk

BASIC INSTINCT

I miss the basic instinct
Before love went extinct
You would be mine
I would be fine
I would be yours
Loving you more
They say obey
You are okay
I am not well
In a bad spell
My spirit loves you
You know it's true
Your spirit loves me
In it completely free
Damn it
Damn this
The rules
The fools
The demands
Like in remand
Why can't I have you
Feel something new
This damn society
This damn anxiety
I got one life to live
One love to you to give
They say I belong there

Not with you, it's not fair
Do we elope?
Will we cope?
Do I just tell the world to go to hell?
Do I just trust my heart where it fell?
Help me, love
Help me come
I am dying inside
Want a ride
Your spirit loves me
In it I am free
My spirit loves you
You know this is true
I have grief
You have belief
I have to have you or die
This I won't lie
My spirit loves you
Your spirit loves me
My spirit
Your spirit
Our spirit
One spirit
One love one spirit

BEAUTY

I looked into the pixels in her eyes
Nowhere did I detect lies
They were a perfect window to a perfect soul
Sees no evil through those eyes at all

I sought to know how she thinks
I looked again through the pixels to the synapses on the brink
Billions upon billions perfectly welded together in circuits
not for thinking of trivia like sweets and biscuits

In the brain itself, I saw bits, bytes, and words well arranged
Everything in thought packets nothing out of range
The speech cued with words of love and affection
Resonance and assonance like a music section

I felt her pulse and traveled to her heart
So much room in her heart love stored without heartache
Atria of her heart fountains of empathy and sympathy
Well insulated against greed, sloth, and apathy

The topological survey of her body
A woman worth to be called somebody
All attributes in the right shape, size, and quantity
A woman of beauty, character, and quality

She died of Covid
Stupid Cupid
I missed her
Should have kissed her.

BIG BURLY BULLY

The big burly bully bullied the poor boy

Forced him to give up his favorite toy

Boy tried not to cry

To be manly he tried

An uppercut cut the bully's trip to Troy

DEAD

He searched for days on end,
deep in his heart's chambers,
for an iota of forgiveness.
There was none.
His aorta spewed renewed anger.
 Enraged every time he thought of the incident.
That incident.

At their usual rendezvous,
at the edge of the park they met.
Young impish boys hardly teenaged
Bundles of perpetual motion
Always causing a commotion.

His sibling brother was there.
Savouring the impossible happening,
possibly the architect of covert instigation.
The big burly bully walked up close, pulled his clothes,
and declared, "I hate you! "

Before he could comprehend from whence the enmity
had derived in his equanimity,
stars were going round his head.
Imaginary birds tweeting in his ears.
Another hard meteoric impact
to his eye and he fell into a deep ditch. Dazed.

A groundsman, watching the scene in disbelief,
came charging to break up the fight. nay,
the drubbing to be honestly honest.

So, there was no reason to forgive.
To forgive the sibling brother for setting him up to
satisfy sadistic pleasures.
No remorse.

So, no wonder he could not forgive.
So, he loathed his sibling brother.
So, loathed him for life.

So, he drove him a knife
Life on ice
Not really nice
Dead.

BLOOD PRESSURE

First day of the month of September
It Will be a day to fondly remember
I became a paid-up full member
My subscription expires on December

I know that by next year March
There won't be much change as such
I will be eating a lot of meat and starch
Eating little carbohydrate for lunch

It has been a hard decision to make
I m a bit of a glutton, I love my steak
But, my blood pressure was at stake
Risking a stroke would be a big mistake

My fitness club is very strict
Though it is the best on the street
They make sure the sweat streaks
Your diet and physique at its peak

I think if I work hard through November
Work from dusk till the sky is amber
I will be fit as a fiddle; out of danger
Fit like Chuck Norris Texas Ranger

BY ANY MEANS

I feel like riding my winnowing basket
Flying in the middle of the night causing harm
I feel like riding my mystical broom stored in my casket
Flying away to torment poor villagers at the farm

My heart has been turned inside out, blood flowing
outside my skin
I feel like hurting someone badly committing a sin
I feel like making progress in my life being horrible
To get what I want by any means possible

I want to really amass wealth and power
For it seems all this talk of a better life is sour
A way to lull me while the smart grab a good life by any
means
For it seems all these prayers shutting my eyes is for
people to pinch

They want to have a head start on a good life
But I m going out there guns blazing wielding a knife
Step out of my way to see the light of day
Step up with money and riches, it's time to pay.

CONFESSIONS 5:1

1.

In the same way I wasn't worried before I was born
I am not worried about what happens when I am dead
and gone
I am worried about my meal for tomorrow
Good thing with God for the past fifty years I never had
to borrow

2.

I am worried about the thermo switch on my CRV
Good thing they are two a penny just need to go see
Ronald Vee
I am worried the rains are late again this season
I am doing things to mitigate, global warming the
reason

3.

The same way I was just a chromosomal swimmer
without conscience
When I die it is not my problem to know what happens
to me its science
All my yearning for life and death knowledge
Is hidden in plain science in storage

4.

If there is heaven it's so nice you live forever then die and go.
We won't be missing you here on earth no no
If there is hell why do you keep talking sin in your confessions
I won't be helping you in your religious sessions

5.

This is the life
Leave that knife
See me in you
I in me I see you
If you love me true
And I love you too
We are one
We are done
God is love
God is love

COVID 19 AND ALL

Rainfall is,
above
below
or normal

Temperature,
humidity,
pressure
can be too

Blood pressure,
blood sugar,
body temperature
Can be
above,
below
or normal

With Covid 19 and all
Are you feeling normal?

COVID KILLS

Politicking while the people perish

Frolicking with death nightmarish

COVID does kill

He gets the thrill

Electioneering win his relish

COVID KILLS (ACROSTIC)

C-an you imagine, people
O-ver the world people dying
V-irus killing them, people crying
I-n most cases those who are feeble
D-emagogue on campaign footing
K-eeps lying that disease is scooting
I-n order to win another election
L-eaving people with wrong selections
L-eading to thousands of lives lost
S-ociety bearing a heavy cost

WHO'S DYING?

What does it profit a man to win an election

but, let people die, and say it is natural selection

Instead of saying it loud and very clear

and, stop spreading despondency and fear

That, we need to all listen to science

We need to shout and not be silent

That, always in public wear a mask

that, personal hygiene is another task

that, social distancing, for now, is good.

Some leaders are busy in election mood,

lying that the statistics are wrong

that, the economy is resilient and strong

that the scientists and doctors are lying,

Just because Blacks, Hispanics, and minorities, mainly,
are dying.

COVID 19

My throat is sore
My head is sore
My heart is sore
My back is sore
My muscles sore
At this rate, I could be no more

I need more care
More fresh air
More tea
More vitamin C
More vitamin D
More to drink or I will be sorer

I need painkiller
A natural healer
A natural thriller
A boredom filler
To avoid this killer
Called COVID 19

COVID ON THE STREET

Change brings opportunity and uncertainty

On my way to the central business district of Harare

Vehicles driving cautiously like they social distance

Intimidated by gun-toting police and army in uniforms
of repression

Driving to S. Machel Avenue I parked my car, adjusted
my face mask

One solitary Parking Marshal appeared at my car
window

No change for my US Dollar so I phoned my wife to send
Ecocash,

The electronic payment platform giving politicians a
hard time.

Hard currency is short so people trade money on their
phones,

Exasperating the Reserve Bank.

They can't control money on the phone

Streets are unusually clean, no beggars, no touts, no
pickpockets

The infamous vendors and street children all driven out
at gunpoint

Reflecting on this it seems heartless but obviously, Covid doesn't care

Everywhere you look there is a roadblock with mean uniformed men,

Enforcing a military junta's unpopular curfew with corruption rife

This is the new reality in Harare, a city of face masks and silence.

DIFFERENT VIEWPOINT

Raise that middle finger in a fiddle
Prickly point makes a people fickle
You just want to talk
Folks want you to walk
Different viewpoint they claim it's a riddle

Different viewpoint

I have a viewpoint
Different than yours
Similar to who knows
I have an opinion
I am not a minion
What do you say?
Maybe I am going astray
I still wanna be heard
You don't like my beard?
But you are extra tall
I don't care at all
If you have something to say
I will say speak you may
I may agree
Disagree
You are free
To say your mind
I may find
A different viewpoint

Different viewpoint

Different viewpoint

D-ead silence
I-s compliance
F-ree to air
F-air is fair
E-njoy freedom
R-eplay
E-very word
N-o bias
T-he basis
V-erbatim
I-n my style
E-very one
W-orld over
P-oint of view
O-n anything
I-s unique
N-o one
T-o stop

A different point of view
A different point of view

FLIGHT OF THE DEAD

In his mind the world at his feet
Everything appearing sweet
He made promises to deliver
Spent sleepless nights in the river
Trying to swim out of promises
All ventures turning to crisis

Insomnia played him at night
He watched the sun bring new light
In his mind demons roamed free
Friends he could no longer see
His freenemies became enemies
Mum and dad his nemeses

When all was said and done
He could no longer face anyone
He wanted to take flight
To go forever out of sight
He took the turn
Point of no return

He took the flight of no return
Flight of the dead
He died
They cried

DEAL WITH THEM

I wish I could have done better
He wishes he had not procrastinated
She wishes she had written the letter
They wish the stream they had not contaminated
We wish we had voted this particular person
The world wishes it had learned a lesson

Things are what they are
Deal with them
Damn!
No use lamenting after
They are what they are
Deal with them

DEAR FAMILY

Dear Barbie Doll, I wanna say I love you in case I pass on. This disease is unpredictable and could have me breathless anytime. It's been 38 years of bliss, from that stolen kiss when you were fifteen. We have gone uphill and downhill together. When you cried I cried. When you laughed I laughed. Now, in our fifties, I wanna say you are still Barbara, my Barbie Doll.

"Mai Bhubha my baby, please be my Barbie. I sing this song just for you, my Barbie. Mai Bhubha ma Barbie, please be my honey. I sing this tune just for you, my baby.

Barbara baby, Barbara baby, Barbara baby, Barbara B.

Barbara baby, Barbara baby, Barbara baby. Barbara be mine."

Dear Bhubha my son,

You have grown up to be quite a handsome young man. An accomplished artist with many fans. I know we have not always been on the same page, but this was just a passing phase. We are similar in many ways and as you know a positive and a positive repel. Whatever misunderstanding was in good standing to make you a father one day and you will.

Son, where are my grandkids? I want so much to spoil them and turn them into rebellious troublemakers just like their father. Perhaps God will allow me to meet them before I breathe my last. Time will tell.

Dear Daughter of the Father,

If I should have my last breath now, due to this virus, I rest assured I have a capable grown-up bambino. A daughter of the father. You wrote a beautiful song at age eight and sang it perfectly. I see both myself and your mum in you. The intelligence from mom, the leadership from me. You will make it. You are a child of the universe and your vibrations will be felt all over the globe.

If ever things don't make sense in your life, get a piece of paper and write a song. Write a poem. Things will clear up.

Keep doing everything and anything as you have always done. I will be there to guide you and rescue you, even from the unknown.

Your one and only,

Dhedhi (Dad)

DEATH

Sorry about your death
The way you left the earth
You screamed all of us deaf
To that, there's no mirth

You are off to hell
This we could tell
Your soul you did sell
All your deal totally smell

You dabbled in witchcraft
Stole parts of aircraft
Dabbled in statecraft
Treated death as a craft

DEGREES

Sam(e)

Dig up your dead degrees
We want to see if you agree
Are you really that mad
Marbles lost just like Sam(e)?

Sam(e)

Some fake degrees are forged by decree
Dangerous illiterates roaming free
Paying for favours
Fake endeavours
Illegal scamming scum treated the Sam(e)

Sam(e)

S-ome
A-dmit
M-anipulating
E-ducation

Sam(e)Degree

I read poems, books, newspapers, and letters
and I sit back and wonder how in the name of God we
have come this far in this world.

My impression is that we all have a certain degree of mental illness, myself included. I am not saying it's good or bad. Sometimes a mental illness gets to levels where a person fails to function normally.

I fail to see how a whole people can believe in the superiority of a particular race and make decisions so important based on a figment. How a whole people have gone to war based on fiction much to the chagrin of the whole world. That to me is a mental illness. Or manufactured consent. Or in technical engineering control systems, a dangerous example of positive feedback.

Then we have religious people who go to war to defend a belief that has no bearing on reality. In their mental delusions, they believe in deity differently than other people. That is an advanced state of mental sickness. One Creator one God one people. Science confirms.

There are people who believe and have people believe that they are seers. That they can see into the future. However, why not see pandemics which descend upon the unsuspecting world. These seers do not see these. They bamboozle you with nebulous claims after the fact.

There are lots of people with mental disorders
The difference is in the degree of disturbance
I am not sure how far gone I am
How many degrees do you have?

Degrees of mental illness
Are we all the Sam(e)?
Truthfully!

DEJA VU

There is a freak happening in life no one understands
Something not spliced in our DNA strands
There are people in situations you meet
You feel like you have met in the street.
You feel like you rehearsed the encounter
The clothes you wear you wore at the counter
What you say you said it then and now
Even the subject about which you meet, but how?
Subconsciously you wonder if this is deja vu
Whether the power of premonition is true
The feeling is so out of the body, so alien
You want to say to your interlocutor "Hey Ellen! "
at the risk of appearing to have lost your marbles
The phenomenon is strange but a marvel
So it is that some of the poets on PH
I have met at the dining hall, the DH
Have I met you somewhere wordsmith?
Yes, you who read my poems like
William Wordsworth?

DESTINY

Last day of September
I'm still a member
On Poem Hunter
Despite my banter
We see in December
If I am not dismembered
Maybe in November
Could be any number
So I won't slumber
And encumber
My encounter
With destiny
Tinny winny destiny

I remember
Pretty Lavender
Was a member
Her skin amber
Full of anger
There was danger
From the father
From the brother
From her sister
Behaved rather
Like her mother
Arguing their destiny
Tinny winny destiny

I am not an offender
Because I am tender
I make some redder
With my rejoinder
Critically stricter
A poetic creature
Rhymes being fitter
Some getting bitter
Poems getting sweeter
Lady, I tweet her
Lover on Twitter
Same poetic destiny
Tinny winny destiny

I have adopted a father
Tim Yerman father
Brother to my mother
D. K Swain male mother
R.M. Smith too old rather
Best friend and brother
Step mother V. Madhulika
Now Ma-Deluke-aah
Baby Anais Voinet my sister
Growing up nice 'n sweeter
Many poems hard hitters
All sharing a destiny
Tinny winny destiny

I have haters
Or people better
From Nether
Lands my sister
Sylvia Frances Chan, I hate her
My poet sister, I m a joker
Don't be a protester
You kept my daughter
For years gave shelter
Continue to nurse her
Daughter of the father
All sharing a destiny
Tinny winny destiny

Not on my lister
You still my sister
You still my brother
You are my mother
You are my father
You are whatever
Where ever
Whenever
Which ever
Never ever
Never never
Same PH destiny
Tinny winny destiny

I have to put a stopper
Behave proper
Behave sober
Not sombre
Not macabre
A bulls hitter
Like a cheater
Who meets her
Sweet talks her
Then treat her
Like Harry Porter
Sharing a destiny
Tinny winny destiny

Tinny winny destiny
One two three four
Tinny winny destiny
Five six seven eight
Tinny winny destiny
Nine ten eleven twelve
Tinny winny destiny
I have to go now
Don't know-how
I take my bow
I wipe my brow
One two three
Four five six
Seven eight nine
Poem all mine

A DISEASE

If I said I love you
Would you say you love me too?
And forget everything else
Follow me to the end of the earth
Restart everything
Even that you are a human being
Love needs commitment
Love needs persistence

If I said I love you
Would you say you love me too
And help me build a home in prose
And write poetry while you pose
All over your body
becoming rhythmically embodied
Love needs harmony
A perfect symphony

I really wanna know
Even if the answer is no

Yeah, if I said I love you
Would you say you love me too
And love me even when I'm invisible
Believing our love invincible
Ignoring all your senses
Having faith in consequences

Love needs faith
Not even a face

If I said to you?
Would you say to me too?
That love me
You want me
You need me
You read me
Love is a disease
That's all there is

DON'T TAKE YOUR LIFE

The world has become small
Nowhere can one country fall
The others not feeling the impact
Even when there's an impasse
Between any two or more nations
It causes concern and commotion
To every country here on earth
We are concerned about Japanese deaths

So, please Japan
Don't take your life
Don't use the knife
Don't kill your wife
Don't end your strife
It's not your right
Keep up the fight
Please Japan

COVID is a serious global disease
All countries affected life not this easy
Africa is not too terribly badly
But we remember Japan Aid sadly
When there was a severe famine in Ethiopia
The rest of the world donated like a utopia
So Japan know your pain is our pain
No need to go berserk, to go insane

Please Japan
Don't take your life
Don't use the knife
Don't kill your wife
Don't end your strife
It's not your right
Keep up the fight
Please Japan

And in NZ
In the UK
In Aussie
The USA
Africa
India
Russia
Patagonia
China
Don't take your life

DOOM AND GLOOM LOOM

I am scared beyond fear,
past shedding a condolence tear.
I am seeing invincible mortals fall.
I walk the earth standing tall,
wondering which hearse will drive by,
carrying another muted soul without even saying bye,
No sound of sirens, no flashing light,
silent processions day and night

Doom and gloom loom
Many headed for the tomb,
many buried before noon

It's now a new digital world,
medical systems unfurled.
With Covid you die or survive,
a one or a zero, no one to revive,
doctors, nurses, hospitals on strike.
Politicians shouting hoarse on the mic,
"Chloroquine, Zithromax, and zinc! "
Mask; wash hands; isolate out of sync.

Doom and gloom loom
Many headed for the tomb,
many buried by afternoon

I have already written my will,
Gone around town, paid my bill
The hysteria is palpable,
our leadership culpable.
To all the poets around the globe
This poet the virus might robe
If I go missing off this forum
In friendship, I extend my forearm

Doom and gloom loom
Many headed for the tomb
Many died before the full moon

Before I go, before I'm silent
Let me do a poem in silence
Write my own epitaph at least
A poem, a verse, a list
"Here lies a confused engineer,
Instead of fixing the engine near,
he was busy writing poems"
"The Engineering Poet"

Doom and gloom loom
Gloom and doom loom

DOWN WITH RACISM (Acrostic)

Do you know science proves everyone came from Africa
Over there, where you are, you are my descendant
Where, then, do you get the temerity to hate me, therefore yourself
New variations of colour all came from me, the Negro

White, yellow, red, orange, and everything in between
In case you doubt do research on where all humans began
The trouble is the factional politics of religion
How it creates stories to control our minds to suit some

Regardless of what science, the real religion which works, says
And, if you doubt science, put a polythene bag over your head
Crash your head on a rotating guillotine
Ingest cyanide, antifreeze, and see if you can pray to save yourself
So, my children, my descendants, my people, let's love one another
My message to you is; Down with racism.

FAIR IS FAIR IN SICKNESS AND IN HEALTH

The propaganda on Covid 19 is furious
Makes me curious
Covid 19 is a worldwide problem
Many countries rushing vaccination programs

Uncle Sam doesn't pass up a chance to display rabid
hatred
Issues travel warnings to Zimbabwe out of morbid
hatred.
South Africa is known and has been the epicenter since
the start
It breaks my Negro heart
when a huge country like the US
throws propaganda potshots to be a nuisance

Just because South Africa has a sizeable white
population, but is doing badly with Covid nineteen,
the professional avowed bully picks on Zimbabwe
because we are a proud black nation he wants to
cartoon

Thank God the truth doesn't change
Even when unnecessary white supremacy enemies act
strange,
fair is fair in sickness and in health
All this hatred because he covets our wealth.

FATE AND FAITH

Fate beyond faith
Faith beyond fate
The dichotomy

There is no doubt we are here
On this earth
Till death

We need good food
We need clean air
We need water

Items in short supply
We need to conserve
To use smart technology

But we spend our time destroying
Using harmful chemicals
Destroying ourselves

On Sundays, we bundle our kids
Dressed well to go to pray
Minding our faith

There is fate beyond faith
To live well while you live
To others love to give

We prefer faith beyond fate
Destroying our world
As if there is another

FAITH MUSK

Faith is dangerous
I am not being cantankerous
Before you shout "Heathen"
Read me out even

Hitler went to war based on faith
For his race of Aryans with a particular face
We know how that ended
German Law has been amended

Colonists went round the world pillaging
Benighting with Bible the heathen in villages
Murder, rape, torture, and war
Contradicting their faith even more

Nine-eleven was caused by religious extremism
The West believes in capitalism expansionism
The perpetrators believing invaders were infidels
The West had faith they could subdue the impudent.

I am afraid of faith
An irrational belief in some fact
Draped in an aura and a face mask
A faith musk

FATHER

My dear departed father, my old man
I feel like talking to you after such a long span
You have been dead since August nineteen seventy-
nine
So my talk is more a soliloquy or a pantomime
You were not the easiest Pa to talk to
Now I am older than you, fifty-six versus forty-two

You were a formidable freedom fighter
You refused to cow in the face of people mightier
The lesson I got from you was to get up stand up
Fight for my rights no matter how tough
It was a pity you passed away on the eve of
Independence
April nineteen eighty your dream came true but you
had ascended
to a place where I could not talk to you until now
We don't have details of your passing but it happened
somehow

I am sure you are tired of turning in your grave
In disappointment and utter disbelief at the knaves
Your, I mean, our freedom fighter friends have changed
They have become detached even estranged
I shall not be saying more at the pain of incarceration
At the risk of history repeating itself dying with
lacerations

just know that your wife, my mother, is well
The struggle, to our children, we continue to explain.

PESTILENCE SPHERES

Spheres used to have music
Now they make you sick
They used to spin in time
Supporting earthly life
Now spheres cause fears
Ending life in tears
Spheres with spikes
People taking a hike
Fearing pestilence spheres

FIGHTING TILL END

A boxer in the ring fought till the brink
Put ink to paper before he could think
Fighting till end
For his stipend
His slink from arena like from a rink

Fighting till end

Tim was a big boxer from the ghetto
But spoke like a lady with a falsetto
When he met a lady beautifully slim
His voice failed him because he was frigidly timid

Fighting till end

First thing is to know the door
In case you need to leave the floor
Gauge the distance
How to escape the instance
Total defeat is obvious
In case you are oblivious
Next time make sure
Gun is ready and secure
The bullets have not been removed
In the night you slept in the next room
Locate your escape route
Leave a possibility of a rout

Even if your skills are said to be good
Never underestimate the other dude
Death comes fighting till the end

FIVE MINUTES TO SIX

Five sonnets to six hundred
It's been a poetic journey of discovery
I learned a lot of styles
Stories that took me many miles
To the time poetry was in its infancy
And that a poem expresses what you fancy
A flight of fancy
Now that I am on six hundred where to?
I have been certified a poet that's true
Who knew?
That I could be a bard
Writing softly and hard
Time will tell
The toll the bell

FOOTSTEPS ON THE PATH TO NOWHERE

I've walked in many footsteps
My father's I could not forsake
He passed away at forty-two
And I lost the footprint of his shoe

I stepped in the shoes of role models
Some poor some moguls
The impact of some of these,
helped me pay my school fees

Now I'm middle-aged
I have turned every page
I am at the stage
I ask myself where my footsteps have led

Footsteps on the path to nowhere
I've been everywhere
On the path to somewhere
Footsteps on the path to nowhere

FORCED RHYMES

Forced rhymes sound forced depending on dialect
Forced crimes sound coerced depending on the district
The English language is so widespread it has evolved so much
Some people even pronounce the word much to sound like a march
Then there is the issue of poetic license in poetry
I am free to rhyme the word poetry with the word poultry
To assist in the mood and message I convey
So freedom to express yourself makes rules nonsense to obey
So I say if you wanna force that rhyme because it tickles your fancy
Go ahead because poetry is not a crime of fencing.
It's an individual mood thing
So my friends have a good fling

FRISKY MONKEY

Feed the free frisky monkey up a tree
You sit under the tree sipping your tea
You doze a little
Monkey does fiddle
Your tea and bread you can no longer see

Frisky Monkey

F-irst thing you see is he looks like you
R-ear is without fur but that's not new
I-n his mind he sees you as a primate
S-o similar to him but always private
K-icks a fuss to get your attention
Y-ou misunderstand his intention
M-onkey just wanna talk to a human
O-ver and over he says who woman
N-ot clear to us but means hello there
K-now he just wants to clear the air
E-nd of the day you ignore him so
Y-ou regret your peace is a no-no!

GLOBAL WARMING

Dark clouds gathering
A restless wind swirling
Trees sighing in anticipation
We are so sure
The rains are here
The signs are clear

Half an hour later.
The sweltering heat is back
The clouds clear
And I fear
It's another dry day
Met Office with nothing to say

There had been a communique
A map looking complicated
Showing a deluge of hailstorms
Rain and possible floods
Possibly even spilling of blood
From Monday, November twenty-third
Nothing happened I am afraid

Global warming is here

"To change with change is the changeless state"
 After three years of drought straight
We have to forget about the rains
And drill boreholes and run water in drains.

There is no use complaining, praying, and blaming God
Nothing ever remains the same; in other areas it's very cold.
To every adverse situation, there is an opportunity
Here is the opportunity for our unity
Unity of purpose to advance to the next stage
Turn on a new agricultural page
We harness groundwater for food
Ignore rainwater it seems for good

Global warming is here.

GOOD TIDINGS

I see visions of a good year coming
And that counts for something
Otherwise, it's been mounds of bad news
A year of bad issues

The world at crossroads
As if we crossed the Lord
Prayers bouncing off deaf ears
Faces drenched in forlorn tears

Sure as the sun rises to set
We expect things to let
We expect no longer to be mournful
We remain hopeful

Where there's life there's hope
So our brows we mope
And look forward to a better life
Good tidings to all mankind

GODCHILDREN

Beloved godchildren
The sun was rising on you
You were going to blossom
You were going to flourish
Counted among children
Tummies full of nutrients
Your future has been clouded
Your opportunities shrouded
Caught up in a mythical belief
You will suffer without relief
I weep for you children
My heart bleeds godchildren

Beloved godchildren
You do not know your father
You do not know why he left
You did not ask to be born
You are just godchildren
You are just grandchildren
The world belongs to you
This science is not new
They are looking for heaven
Heaven is not the real haven
Cry, beloved godchildren
I weep for you godchildren

GREENER SCENE

Cleaner cleans river full of pollution
Greener scene on earth a revolution
This our only home
Earth our only hope
Polluter eats paper as a solution

Greener scene

Go green all over
Recycle all paper
Every plastic
Every elastic
Nonferrous stuff
Even steel tuff
Recycle recycle
Send bicycle
Control our death
Earth is our earth
Never pollute
Every one resolute

Greener scene

We want a grinner scene. Everyone was seen smiling. For that scene to be seen we need to recycle a greener scene. Don't drive to arrive, cycle that bicycle. You will be fitter and lady ozone not bitter, about how you treat her, belching stuff at her visage like a mirage in the Arabian Desert. Scientists, those pesky factual mathematically modeling fiddling meddling busybodies, have said it. The attention we haven't paid it. That energy cannot be created or destroyed but transformed from one form to another. So tell your mother that rather than using firewood to cook that meal for your father, brother, and sister, rather, she must use renewable energy; that rather than in her lovely garden; put artificial toxic harmful chemicals like paraquat, she must use organic stuff. Organic manure will pamper, pep up, and prevent the poisoning of the environment ensuring a fair chance for every organism, big and small, to survive. For power, use solar, except in the Polar Regions where the sun sleeps most of the time. It is a crime against humanity to pile grime in climes all time zones included. Nothing is excluded, whether extruded or extended. Some have tended to find excuses, something about quarters blah blah blah. We don't want stories. Stop polluting! Use renewable energy!

I have used up my energy ranting. Rest, me, be granting. Let us not be found wanting. Don't destroy our planet. "The Planet of Apes" and human beings and all living things.

H. & L. R US

Never you feel down
Uncle Deluke's in town
He stands his ground
Anointed village clown

When times are rough
The going getting tough
He is there with enough
Enough jokes to make you laugh

Why you carry the world?
Carrying His cross you failed
Even when He cried and wailed,
watched on the cross He nailed

So cast imaginary demons away
You don't even have to pay
Come out let us joke and play
Uncle Deluke's humour here to stay

The demons of mental morbidity
Have super psychological mobility
Imposing multiple personalities on the world
Civility, congeniality, nobility unfurled

Know that Humour & Laughter R Us
Every day riding the humour bus
Never deliberately causing fuss
Because in God Almighty we trust

H.I.M

Though you may make us kneel before you who have no knees we bow down to one Father. Our father is God the creator of you and I and one day you will answer to Him, my Father, why you killed H.I.M killing me

HALLELUJAH!

She came from the east
A hungry beast
Everything in its way bowed, fell, died
Special foundations, to be special, tried
Buffeted once from the east
Anything still standing she would return stronger,
longer, for the feast
Buildings
Bridges
Multi-storey
Same story

I built my hope upon a rock
My faith in the Lord
They denied me space
My race
My face
Out of place
This was my saving grace
My ace
My home never torn
In a perfect storm.

Hallelujah!

HAPPINESS IS HAPPINESS

Happiness has no age
Is the opposite of rage
Happiness has no race
Is obvious on every face
Happiness has no borders
Spontaneous without orders
Happiness is sweet
Uplifts the mood on the street
Happiness reduces stress
You don't need a mistress
Happiness has no magnitude
Longitude nor even latitude
Enjoy every moment of happiness
Happiness is happiness

HAPPY HOUR

Happy hour happy hour
Happy hour I feel the power
Happy hour I am like a flower
Happy hour in my ivory tower

It is not the hour of imbibing
It is not a good wine I m describing
Or at the pub when beer is half price
Or when I am served chicken and rice

It is not when a pastor's speech touches my heart
When I understand creation from the start
When at the synagogue I am in heaven in advance
Nor the feeling of completeness God may grant

Neither is it the quality time I spend
Riding waves, taking the sharp bend
The thrill, the rush, the surge of adrenaline
All splashed up, not a care or worry for my melaninie.

My happy hour when I write a rhyme
My happy hour when I write a stanza
My happy hour when I write a verse
My happy hour when I write a POEM

That is my happy hour
My happiest happy hour

HEAR ME AGE

I used to be so fit
Feared in the street
Everywhere I went
They cleared the way
"Bouncer was coming! "
Everyone screaming, running
Afraid of my rage
Now, you hear me age

I creek like going up a creek
They stand their ground in the street
I move out of the way
I wobble and sway
They taunt me
Remembering days I was mean
Friends laugh I say
Now, you hear me age

My feet swell
In my head a bell
My feet I drag
Walking with a swag

Now, you hear me age
You hear me age
Hear me age
Hear me age

HIDDEN IN OUR EDEN

When we were young I promised
To take her to an island of romance
Where we would only be two
And this has come true
In our old age
We have reached the stage
We live on our own
With our cats and dogs in our home
Our kids are grown and gone
We zoom on the phone
When I said those words forty years ago
Didn't know what I meant, I know
Now I know wishes do come true
In unexpected breakthroughs
Here we are
On our island so far
She cooking seemingly all the time
Sunday chicken
While I do a Sunday afternoon rhyme
Hidden in our Eden.

HUMAN

You may be rich preach teach or cheat
You may be Burmese, Chinese, Japanese
You may be bright, white, mighty
You may be Indian, West Indian, Red Indian
You may be African, American, Jamaican
Black, white, yellow, pink, brown, or even orange

We are human
All born of woman
Covid 19 has shown us
We are on the same bus

When a person gets sick and dies
Don't ignore their misery and cries
When a person is hungry and poor
Don't ignore them and close the door
When a person different than you
Faces any challenge it is still true

We are human
All born of a woman
Covid 19 has shown us
We are on the same bus

Human
From a woman
Be human, please do
Human be true

HUMAN RELATIONSHIPS MAY BE LIKE THAT

The so-called evil person may be the one who is good
The most intolerant may be the person who preaches tolerance
The one they label bad may be the most loving person.
Human relationships may be like that.

The most intolerant may be the person who preaches tolerance,
Stands in front pontificating with a forked tongue
Human relationships may be like that.
It is foolish to allow another mortal to control your soul,

Stands in front pontificating with a forked tongue
The one they label bad may be the most loving person
It is foolish to allow another mortal to control your soul
The so-called evil person may be the one who is good

I

When I die
I won't cry
I shan't
I can't
I ll be in rigor mortis
Tears of the living won't notice
Having gone
To sleep alone
No regrets
'Twas as good as it gets
No dull moments
Lots of comments
Now silent
In my islet
Six feet down
No longer in town

I would remember
January to December
Every month
Enjoying so much
Every day of the week
Pleasure at its peak
Monday was money day
Robbing people of their pay
Tuesday was the day we'd choose them
Those to rob without shame

Wednesday was weddings day
At weddings pretending to pray
Thursday we would be thirsty
Ready for the next day's feisty
Friday we roast them with beers
Beef, chicken, the opaque, the clears

Saturday was the start day we'd be at our peak
A day of counting the blessings of the week
Sunday was a fun day
Getting ready for Monday
A full life
Doing what I like
So when I die
I'll just sigh
My last breath
My final break
No ceremony
No sermon
'Twill just be me
I'll be free
Dying
I

COUNTING ON THE FACT

Covid nineteen is almost as good as a death sentence
Doesn't afford enough time for repentance
It depopulates
Discombobulates

I am counting on the fact that
I wear a mask
I sanitize
I keep a distance

I am counting on the fact that
Everyone is in the game
And will do the same
We are each other's keeper

I am counting on the fact

I AM EVERY HUMAN

I am every human
A man even a woman
Even an animal I can be
I am a poet I am free

I can be in any situation
Right at the beginning of creation
Even in the future I can be
A poet sees what we can't see

I can be with angels sweet
The devil doing bad on the street
Or an alien you cannot see
As a poet, I can live in the sea

I have my poetic license
I cannot tolerate silence
I carry the voice of everyone
A poet can be anyone

So when I read like I know you
When my poem reads so true
I can be *she* or you man
I am a poet I am every human

I am every human

I AM PERFECT NOW

I could never do anything right

You always wanted me out of sight

I was even responsible for your flatulence

Even though you were ill with incontinence

Every one of your miseries

Was due to me not your usury

Even when the weather was inclement

You blamed me for your debts' increment

Now that you have caused my demise

There is nothing for you to demand

Your secret will rot with my carcass

No one will know you caused my car crash

I m too deep to hear your thunder

I m perfect now lying six feet under

I LOVE POETRY

For life to have a meaning something must occupy you
This is fundamentally essential to create hope in life
You have got to have something which drives you
Something you look forward to in your life

I have got my plot where I farm
I enjoy that but it's not the ultimate
I could have joined some church
For some political mind games
I could have found another hobby
But at my age options are limited

Don't get me wrong
The bond with my wife is strong
We live a happy comfortable life
We outgrew our childish strife

Our kids grown
Both gone
Doing their life thing
Wife and I on the scene

The martial way of life is over
There is a new life order
The principles and philosophy linger
But no more push-ups on one finger

The restless spirit though remains till the end
That cannot be replaced not even by a friend
It's a journey I make alone in my mind
I feel on this journey peace I find

Looking back there's not much I haven't done
I been there, done this, had fun
I have done all combinations of booze
I realized with booze I lose
I have even owned a nightclub
The surreal nocturnal life playing dumb
Even ran for national office
The corruption and intrigue made me come off it
I am still a community leader
But that is small at least I get a breather

The only thing which sparks my interest is poetry
Poetry is therapy
It makes me cheer up
My health has improved
It is highly approved
I have reduced my hypertension drugs from three to
one
Even that one I will soon get rid off
Every morning I wake up around four
I write a poem title on my phone
Sometimes a poem is spontaneous
Sometimes it takes time to make it momentous
Then I do ten to fifteen minutes of exercise
Squats, dumbbell lifting, and hand grippers

Then bath and off to work
To labour and sweat
Being the owner and my own boss
I write poetry making sure there is no business loss

My evening is poetry
My day at work is poetry
When I drive around I see poetry
When I fail to sleep I write poetry
Poetry poetry poetry
I love poetry

Psychologists say too much of anything is bad
I ask would they rather I do something mad
They even have a name to make it sound heavier
Obsessive-compulsive behavior
My genetic makeup makes me restless
I just can't sit around doing nothing so this is baseless
What a noble and harmless way to spend the day
I am too opinionated to have nothing to say
What better way to speak than through poetry
I can let my imagination go wild with poetry

I can offend with poetry
Apologize, amend with poetry
I can move you with poetry
Connect with you in poetry
Poetry poetry poetry
I love poetry

I DON'T UNDERSTAND

I don't understand why you don't understand
We have been given a once in a lifetime opportunity to live
Billions of spermatozoon would have wanted a chance
You triumphed thrived survived and lived

We have been given a once in a lifetime opportunity to live
Why then do you say this place is not your home?
You triumphed thrived survived and lived
Are you not better placed to live, love and bequeath the future?

Why then do you say this place is not your home?
Billions of spermatozoon would have wanted a chance
Are you not better placed to live love and bequeath the future?
I don't understand why you don't understand.

I OFTEN WONDER

I was thinking
I was drinking
My coffee
Eating toffees
What drives a bard
To write a ballad
A verse
Being not averse
To things subjective
Using adjectives
Is it to influence?
To find a confluence
Of ideas
For certain ideals
Maybe to draw tears
For things done over the years
The world doesn't change,
Though it's strange,
because a poet writes a piece
He doesn't find peace
People don't care
though not fair
Whether what you write is the truth
There is still no truce
Life goes on
A poet on his own
Writing life experiences

Unique occurrences
For what?
So that what?
Is it the love of rhyme?
Or just wasting time?
My mind wanders.
I often wonder

I, COVID 19

I am laughing out loudest.
My name is Covid nineteen
These days I am the proudest
People feel me but I can't be seen
I have caused so much hysteria
Making people sick like diphtheria
Everyone in quarantine
Panic I'm guaranteeing

I've been around for a century
Some are playing the blame game
I tasted effluent and mercury
So blaming someone is lame
I moved to bats and pangolins
Then onto meat eaten by mandarins
Now I cause chest damages
I live in human lung passages

I know humans will succeed
Humans are fighting back
To starve me of my feed
Make no mistake there is a backlash
I will have to find a new host
Humans no good as ghosts
I am, I, Covid nineteen
Causing mayhem never seen

IN TIMES LIKE THESE

In times like these, you value your loved ones
Realizing how easy it is to lose them
You set aside your little fights and tiffs
And just cherish those moments of bliss

So it was today with my soul mate
Went shopping together usually I would hate
We hardly shop together because I don't understand.
Why she goes through all the hypermarket stands

So this Saturday the nineteenth of October twenty
twenty
We shopped isle by isle together like we have money
plenty
It's been a while felt good like something new
And I realized that what people say is true

They say you don't appreciate something or someone
till they are gone
I wanna appreciate my closest companion in my home
What better way than let her shop at will
From isle to isle we hopped right up to the till
Checking prices but not always buying
Cherishing every moment realizing we are not yet dying

To every couple married or not
I just wanna say give a thought
to your partner's annoying quirks
his or her little personal traits
And enjoy these strange times together
You never know when they may leave you forever.

IDEAS

They came in their thousands
Taking me to the town's end
Some were quite vicious
Some a bit more judicious
Most were completely outrageous
Some virulent and contagious

I found myself at crossroads
Like I was doing a difficult crossword
Puzzled by the relentlessness
Causing me severe breathlessness
My head was pounding
Pressure mounting

What was I to do
With so many ideas all new
I went to bed
To rest my head
Too many ideas
Ideas

I REST MY CASE

All those who imply there are taboo subjects raise your
hand
That in poetry there are subjects out of bounds I don't
understand
Just switch off
If you are afraid of
A subject
An object
A project
An edict

Happiness is when I go there
To discuss things that are rare
To make you sit back and wonder
To make your mind wander
If long-held beliefs are true
Me and you
Stereotypes
The hypes

Happiness is when I do poetry
When a subject I portray
In an unexpected fashion
Cause some to fuss on
an issue never broached
Never approached
I rest my case
And self efface

INSOMNIA

Today I am very very grotty
Tried to sleep but sleep I could not-ly
I tossed and turned
Many candles burned
Scared of witches hoity-toity

INSOMNIA

I- tried to catch forty winks
N-ot as simple as you think
S-tars kept me company tonight
O-ver the moon the cow tried
M-ooing and jumping till I sleep
N-ot a chance eyes awake I keep
I-n the morning the cheerful sun
A-gain blew out my candle pun

GOODNIGHTS

Shrinks say it is a debilitating disease,

but I go through it severally with ease

Listening to the changes in the mood of the night

The hoo hoo hooting owl feeling alright

I can hear night dwellers gleefully coming out

Making a mockery of my wish for silence I just wanna shout

A cicada doing its utmost to compete with a cricket

Late-night imbibers staggering home on their feet rickety.

I try to play videos in my mind to bore my brain to sleep

All I do is scare myself awake some more with horror scripts.

Then by the dead of night, it becomes deathly silent.

Like all creatures great and small are scared of a tyrant.

Like all creatures great and small have no insect and human rights.
As for me, all I wish for and look forward to, are good nights.

JOKING

For those who wish me dead
Don't be misled
No one dies twice
Not even thrice
When that day comes
When the morgue ups its thump
I go
I know
Don't wish me ill
Don't get me killed
It's not your job
You're just a snob

Those who wish me well
That is swell
I am happy
Let me be crappy
Say its not your decision
These pains like an incision
When time's up
I'll be on Whatsapp
For now
Just bow
Mind your business
Your cheesiness

For those who don't care

You are so rare
It's not fair
To make you share
The same attitude
You're ultimately rude
All the same
It's a real shame
You are ambivalent
So I give your equivalent
Since you don't care
You're stoic like a bear

I m just joking
Some fun poking
Love you all
There's no pall
If I am to die
I'll let you cry
So every one
Don't you worry
It's just Deluke
Having a look
At how funny
He can be punny

IT'S ALL GOOD

It is good that things change sometimes for the bad
I am happy at the change though it may be sad
The stillness of life would cause a boredom movement
The constant change remains our only hope for
improvement
The unexpected always bringing change
Even death and taxes variably strange
So I shan't be surprised that yesterday today feels
normal
And next week last week will feel abnormal
Even the blind see the unfaithfulness of time
The deaf hear the variable timbre of life
Even love becoming hate
The unbecoming fate
It's all good
Well understood.

SCRIPTURES STRICTURES

Strictures caused by scriptures restraining my soul
Sisters, Brothers refraining from it all
Hear the whole truth
Do not be uncouth
"Over the hills and everywhere" you fall

Scriptures strictures

Sunday has come again
Coming with the "Amen! "
Rest in peace my Jesus
In time you will come for us
People haven't changed
They are still acting strange
Under their delusions
Reading many resolutions
Endlessly reciting scriptures
So much causing strictures
So much misunderstanding
Totally lacking understanding
Reading does not lead to leading
In the mind is faith bleeding
Causing consternation
To all people and nations
Under no circumstance did you read
Reading you knew did not fill the need

Everyone just needs to love another
Sorry, today we hate, we kill one the other.

Scriptures and strictures

Scriptures
Strictures
Tricksters
Sisters
Misters
Mind twisters
Thieves
Leave us
We need love
To go above
Recite
Excite
Incite
Incest
Interest
Not best
Lest
We blessed
You messed
Best
Quest
Test
We protest
Conquest
The greatest
Is love
Just love
Ain't nothing to it

No miracle feat
Treat
All street
You meet
Greet
Retreat
Defeat
Ego
Negro
Igloo
Who knew
Who are you?
Truth
It's true
Truce
Juice
Is love
Just love
LOVE
LOVe
LOve
Love
lovE
loVE
lOVE
LOVE
LOV
LO
L......

LA POESIE EST DANS LA RUE

La poesie est dans la rue
Oui monsieur elle est dans la rue
Oui madame elle est dans la rue

La poesie et dans la rue
All over the place as you do your stuff there is poetry
Open your mind to it don't give it rules

Oui madame elle est dans la rue
A pretty lady with a t-shirt written "WOW" across her
bust is a poem
Just write satirically don't make it crude

Poetry is on the street
When you are parked in front of a bar with a billboard
that says "Drink responsibly"
Your poetic mind writes a poem in retreat

Yes Sir and Madam poesy is in the street
Look everywhere on cars, newspapers and in your
experience and your mind
A poet will capture life as he sees it on the beat.

And when you have no inspiration this is what you do
Get a piece of paper, smartphone, or laptop and write
that you lack ideas
Je pense que la poesie est dans la rue
Oui, la poesie est dans la rue

PLANET OF POETS

I wanna take flight far away from my earthly abode
All aboard on a sojourn, few will want my
companionship
Onboard a cruise on the loneliest saddest but a joyous
journey.
On the wings of my imagination
There I will live among a tribe of poets

There I shall live among cohorts who never open their
mouths
Having intercourse by way of verses stanzas and
paragraphs.
I shall build my poetry book in the nooks of my
metaphoric subconscious.
There among the aboriginal proverbs most holy.

Proverbs devoid of literal verbosity. We shall
found our fond homes in pages of literature with sages
residing in our ganglia

Not a word spoke. A world made up of volumes
and volumes of recitals of a mentally deranged scribe's
sonnet, whose sole purpose for non-existence in the
real world is to rebel against hate speech.
To rebel against narcissistic perverted bigots
whose sole purpose for inhaling and exhaling is hatred.

They hate everything. They hate the sky. They hate the sun. They hate the earth upon which nourishment they grow. They hate their progeny. They hate themselves. The reason I cannot fathom.

Do not follow me to my world. Do not trace my steps. You won't pick up the route. Your earthly sniffer canines, the K9, K18, K whatever; know that they will never find me. In my planet of poets.

LEAVING VERY SOON

I am suffering the ineptitude of the multitude
Their misunderstanding and their retrogressive attitude
They have no idea money and time are tightly knit
One causatively affecting the other every bit.
Some pretend to work with you
Behind your back call you a fool
They pretend to be cooperatively assisting
But cast aspersions and your goals shifting

Ingrates are mentally paralyzed
never stopping to get their blessings analyzed
Where do you get a leader so committed?
His own life and pleasures omitted
Spends his time and money and assets
Working to better the collective lot to assert
their right to a better life in the land of their birth
Their only God-given home on this earth.

It's like they have a right
To your time
patience all fine
money in kind
assets all mine
They think I owe them a living
Leeches lulled into believing
I am there, won't be leaving.

But I am leaving very soon
Back to my cocoon.

LET THE MUSE PLAY

We have crossed different rivers
Different things life gives us
Some have seen war
Others have had peace more

I think if we read a poem
Emotions a poet wants to pour 'em
We might find an aspect disgusting
Even sometimes debasing

This is how we become a citizen of the world
Having different stories unfurled
In prose and verse
Let us not be quick to judge and be averse

Let the muse play
Let the poet, poetess have their say
It is the poet, the poetess's day
Let the muse play

LIFE AND DEATH

Each to his solitude in times like these
No scope for flocking like geese
Whatever happens in your aloneness
See you on the other side

If you take your last breath
Due to a heavy burden under your breast
Our times may be synchronized
See you on the other side

If you are destined to reincarnate
You are one of the fortunate
You will be pleasantly surprised
When I see you on the other side

If you are headed straight to the Father
And there's no place other
Do not be shocked to find me there
See you on the other side

If you are going to join the food chain
All the other options are in vain
I shall be there with you soon
See you on the other side

And if it so happens you survive
You sanitize, wear a mask, get sick, and be revived
I shall follow the lead of your example
See you on the other side.

One world
One hope
One people
One destiny

Life and death

LIFE IS A CYCLE

It would not be life if everything remained the same
Sadness laced with happiness
Death giving us life

It would not be weather if the seasons did not change
Hot to cold
Dry to wet

It would not be a day if a light was not stolen by
darkness
You wake to work
Sleep to rejuvenate

We would not be human if we did not err
Doing right wrongly
Wrongly doing right

We would not be in love if we did not have lovers tiffs
A misunderstanding here
An irritation there

Life is a cycle
Today it's mine
Tomorrow your time.

LIFE IS EVERYWHERE

If you have water
You will have life
Even when its a little hotter
Organisms will thrive
Life factors are everywhere
Life is everywhere

Those who think humans are unique
Your thinking is oblique
Among the billions of planets
You reckon only earth has clarinets?
There is life somewhere
Life is everywhere

Our spaceships need improving
So that even with the gravity they are cruising
Going faster and faster
Lasting longer and longer
Then we will find life everywhere
Life is everywhere

Instead of having philosophical arguments
Depleting life with war entanglements
Let's keep researching propulsion for life
Whether we can teleport or use a kite
To find ET before it finds us anywhere
Because life is everywhere

LIFE IS.....

Life is so precious
A bubble by a bubble maker
You blink
It's gone
Torn
Flown
Gone like the wind
Gone indeed

Inside the bubble
A bundle
Dreams and hopes
An imaginary hoax
But it's real
You feel
Joy and pain
An insane train

Life is so so precious
Love it
Enjoy it
Give it
It's short
Give it a good shot
Live it
Then leave it

This life
Sometimes nice
The strife
The knife
May strike
You don't like
You die
That's life

LISTEN!

Poetry is not politics
Both are a play on words
Poetry dances with words for posterity
Politics claims they do for prosperity
How come politicians are hard on bards?
Poetry tells (a good poem) as it is
Giving fake lying politico's unease
Each to his calling
Politicians falling
Poets writing in derision
Mocking politician's decisions
At the reception the deception
Politician pontificates blah blah blah
The poet captures the blatant blammy
No love lost
No boast
I want to be an honest poet
Not a f#$*@sh×-*¥ politician

LITTLE BIRD

Every morning when I wake up
A bird sings me different tunes
It's the same bird perched up a tree
I have tried to look up I can't see

Some days at four in the morning it sings
A joyful tune which to me sounds like
"Brother Dhiva has come! Brother Dhiva has come"
Brother Dhiva was my mechanic who will never come
He is late now succumbed to something
He was always late coming for appointments
When he arrived the little bird would sing to my
amazement

On some days the sonorous bird changes tune
While I am sitting wondering what rhyme to use
What point of view I wish to put in a poem
The little bird I never see talks to me.
"You are pure evil. You are pure evil"
Or so I hear when I fill in the syllables
I soul search to see if I had done anything bad
Then I remember the holocaust and I feel sad.

The little bird has so many different tunes
I always wonder what courtship message it croons
Whatever it is communicating to someone
I always wake up full of poetry and love

Thank you little bird.
Though your music is weird
I look forward to your sermon
Tells me I am alive in the morning.

LOGIC AND REASON TOOK A HOLIDAY

Logic and reason took a holiday
The day we accepted a ceasefire
We were making advances every day

We were making advances every day
The enemy was about to be defeated
He now understood we had something to say

Logic and reason took a holiday
When at his doorstep we silenced our guns
Thinking he had had enough pounding Monday to
Monday

We were making advances every day
He appeared to surrender in order to regroup
Here we are again disagreeing day after day

Logic and reason took a holiday
When we decided to give peace a chance and forgot;
"He who fights and runs away lives to fight another day"

The dreaded event came on May Day
When we took up arms again
We were making advances every day
Logic and reason took a holiday

LONELY MOMENT

There is something subliminally beautiful about solitude,

When space and time for you are secluded,

Your volume completely surrounded by yourself,

Like a library book forgotten on a demolished library shelf,

Whose silent chapters envelop the whole space.

Truths and lies in this state come face to face,

Full of memories and stories blank to your mind.

There are many shades and hues of loneliness,

Sleep, comma, lone walk, detention, but the best kind,

Is when you lie six feet under on your way to His Holiness?

The best of the best of a lonely moment,

Far, far away from all worldly comment

When you are tired of the din, the sin, the torment,

Embrace the endless quietude of this lonely moment.

LONGING TO BE HEARD

I sit down and listen all-day
They think I have nothing to say
Like only they are able to pray
I nod my head in fake acquiescence
longing to be heard

The men say because I am a female
I am not allowed to speak at sermons
I know their pastor is a shemale
They ignore me for their acquaintance, but I m longing
to be heard

I see the young adolescents waiting
The teenage boy misunderstood paining
My grandparents' old fashioned straining
Husband, wife, girl or boy friend, everyone,
longing to be heard

Someone listen before it's too late
Unlistening has sealed many a fate

LOST CAUSE

Guy without cause lost pose because of those
Those in who powerful power repose
Tried a coup the cost
Tried campaign he lost
Worked for the one he had tried to depose

Lost cause

A man lost his pose because of his girth
His friends always laughed at him since birth
At the annual contest (he was an alien)for refugees
He decided to submit a portrait of his effigy.

Lost cause

L-osing is part of winning
O-ne wins due to scheming
S-hame befalls the loser
T-he loser the accuser
C-ausing embarrassment
A-ccusing winner of embezzlement
U-ntil people get tired of the circus
S-illy accusations of hoccus poccus
E-very loser knows it's a lost cause

THE LOUD SILENCE

Do me those AC/DC earbuds fast fast
The silence is too loud a blast
I feel the decompression badly
Like a plane dropping altitude madly

My engineering ears love the noise
The clunk clunck part of my poise
When my eardrums stop vibrating
The loud silence gets my brain gyrating

Somebody say something anything
Somebody do something vibrating
The loud silence is really killing
I miss the din-din tin tin really trilling

Doesn't help I been a bad boy
I've had all my muse and my noise toy
Taken away I'm in purgatory detention
Getting the silent treatment intentionally

Help me overcome the loud silence

LOVE ME!

Yesterday I met the spirit of ubuntu
The ancient spirit making me black
It extolled me to remain focused and true
Said in my blackness there's nothing I lack
I should remain steadfast in my soul
There was nothing nothing at all
that which restrained me from kindness
That it is only in my mind, is found my blindness

For years I have been meeting Jesus
He calls upon me in times of need
That Judeo gentleman who forgives us
He has shown me revelations and their biblical seeds
Regularly he tells me to not read anything
That reciting and knowing leads to nothing
He tells me about the need for love
Says only by loving once, loving twice, and loving allows,
I go above

Now I met you
A spirit so pure so new
Give me love
Spirit of love
Love me
Love Me!

LOVE TIMETABLE

Since I was born
Spent years on my own
No one to phone to love
No one home to come
To have to hold or scold
Blankets I do fold when cold

Till we met at the table
I was able
To have my life stable
And a love timetable

You are my hon
Twice in the morn
Thrice I phone
Get your favourite corn
My love you've won
Had dinner for one

Till we met at the table
I was able
To have my life stable
And a love timetable

OBSESSION

You are so hot I m afraid when you touch me
spontaneous combustion will consume me.
When you are happy I feel the giddiness of your
salubrity
When you are sad I feel the weight of lead in my soul.
When you sleep I feel the serenity of heaven in my soul
When you stare at me I feel my mind oscillating in
simple harmonic motion.
When I watch you walk I see the dance of a thousand
angels
When you tell me you love me my heart plays a
beautiful arpeggio in the key C Major.
But the best feeling envelopes me when you immerse
me in your warm embrace in the solitude of our
loneliness.

Tell me, are you born of a woman or God fashioned you
with his own hands.
Tell me when you walk how come I do not hear your
footsteps as you float on a carpet of air.
Tell me, if I was to write you a love letter are there
enough words to convey what I feel. Nay, do I need the
tongues of all the twelve tribes of Isreal to make you
understand how I feel.
Tell me, would you blame me if I committed the sin of
cannibalism, if, God forbid, you left me for another
man. For, if I can't have you I will make sure, my love,

that no one else can. I would rather assimilate you than lose you. I am not just in love with you, but I am compulsively obsessively in love with you. Without you, the world ends.

MASKS AND FEARS

Masquerading
Parading
Money
With honey
Ignoring monsoon
Coming soon
The pestilence
The persistence

Triolette of hoity toity
Haute hippie faulty
Three musketeers
Free master bearers
Breathing free
The pollen from the tree
Contaminated
Concatenated

Musketeers
Masks and tears
Be wise
Sanitize
End of day
Nothing to say
Caskets and tears
Masks and fears

TUNE OF MELANCHOLY

There is music everywhere
Rendering every soul bare
Songs in scales major
Blues blown scales minor
Cacophony of sounds
All over doing rounds
In this world
Emotions unfurled
Eardrums in constant motion
Brain sound processor in commotion
People playing upon a harp
Till their fingers feel harm
Alas, there is no spiritual harmony
On earth a tune of melancholy
I am sending 5 more to give you a choice on what goes
with the book title best.

MIDNIGHT SIGHS

An owl, hoots, closed one eye, sighs, and sleeps.
The mouse finally going to look for nuts
A big sigh of relief that the guy with fake horns is
nodding.
There is no sign of the snake, tonight.
What a sigh of relief for rodents
Except that the reptile is sated having given a large toad
its last sigh
Mom and dad heaving a huge sigh of relief-
the baby is finally asleep at mid
night
their new dog is barking giving them relief from burglars
At last, they can practice family planning in solitude
Sighs everywhere
Midnight sighs.

MISSING YOU

If I should ever go to a mental hospital
It will be because I miss you so much
If you should find me scaling a vertical wall
It will because I am trying to find you
If you should find all flowers without petals
It's me going, 'She loves me she loves me not'
If you should find the local stream with tributaries
It will be the tears I shed for you
Missing you
Kissing you.
If you should find my home razed to the ground
Know that I am not longer around
Gone up in flames
And you to blame.

MOB PSYCHOLOGY

There is oncology
Geology
Genealogy
Gynecology
Etymology
Egyptology
The most dangerous "ology"
Is mob psychology

In a community
There's herd immunity
Security
Maturity
Sometimes futility
Fertility
The threat to all these "ility"
Is lack of social mobility

It is mob psychology
Futility in psycho-analogy
Instead of change utility
People engage in hostility
To programs of hospitality
Exposing their imbecility
Even their futile spirituality
leads to futility and scarcity

Mob psychology
Is bad psychology
Is sad psychology
Is mad psychology
Is sob psychology
Is snob psychology
Is odd psychology
Is mob psychology.

BLINDSPOT

How could I not see you
Shining anew
A star
Dazzling from far
Your love washing me
But I could not see
Even your beautiful scent
A hundred percent
Exciting but I walked away
Now I have pay
For my blind spot
My imperfect dot
My blind spot
Blindspot

Hearts on a collision course
My fault of course
Should have looked left, then right
Should have kept you in my sight.
Should have looked behind
In a bind
A quick glance
The only chance
In the mirror
My error
I saw
Nothing more
In my blind spot
My blind spot

ABOUT THE AUTHOR

DELUKE MUWANIGWA

I was born on June 18, 1964 in southern Zimbabwe, in a village called Chivi, in Masvingo Province. At the time, Zimbabwe was under Ian Smith's government and a guerrilla war was in its infancy to free the country from colonial rule. I have scant memories of my early days, but the difficult rural life and occasional abuses I went through, stir sad memories in me sometimes. Some of it is captured in my poems.

In 1973 I moved to Zambia to escape the escalating bush war. In December 1977 my father inexplicably decided to immigrate back to the then

Rhodesia at the height of the war and his nationalist activism eventually took his life in August 1979.

On April 18, 1980, Zimbabwe got its Independence from Britain. At that point, I went back to school to repeat my grade seven, passed, and went to Lord Malvern High School, in Waterfalls, a suburb of Harare, where I met my wife. Our affair started when we were in form two in 1982, she being 15 years old and I, being 18 years old.

We were in the same class for the 6 years of our secondary school, passed well, and went to the University of Zimbabwe. I studied electrical engineering and she studied pharmacy.

We are still together today, nearly 40 years later. We have two children, Dananayi and Mudiwa Nathasia.

The question on many peoples' minds may be; what's an electrical engineer doing writing poetry?. Beats me, but, it's something I have a natural passion for. I did not go to poetry school, though I wish I had, and I have learned poetry the hard way; through reading poetry and interacting with other poets on poetry fora. Enough said. Enjoy the poems.

www.ingramcontent.com/pod-product-compliance
Lightning Source LLC
LaVergne TN
LVHW010524200726

843506LV00013B/2703